WEATHER PATTERNS

CLIMATE CHANGE

by

Harriet Brundle

THE SECRET BOOK COMPANY

©2020
The Secret Book Company
King's Lynn, Norfolk PE30 4LS

ISBN: 978-1-78998-118-6

Written by:
Harriet Brundle

Edited by:
Charlie Ogden

Designed by:
Drue Rintoul

A catalogue record for this book is available from the British Library.

CONTENTS

Words in **bold** are explained in the glossary on page 31.

WHAT IS CLIMATE CHANGE?

KEY TERMS

- The <u>weather</u> is the day-to-day changes we see and feel outside. For example, the weather may be sunny in the morning and raining in the afternoon.

- The <u>climate</u> is the usual weather in a place over a longer period of time. For example, Antarctica has an extremely cold climate for most of the year.

- <u>Climate change</u> is the long-term change in the climate and usual weather patterns of an area. Climate change usually affects very large areas. It could be a change in the amount of rainfall or the average temperature of an area.

Earth's climate is always changing. Over the last 4.5 billion years, Earth has experienced both very hot and very cold climates. For the last 11,000 years, Earth's climate has stayed at a stable temperature of around 14°C. However, in recent years this average temperature has been slowly increasing.

Tropical climate

Arctic climate

Why Might a Climate Change?

There are many different reasons for why a climate might change.

Some changes to climates throughout history have had natural causes, for example **volcanic eruptions**. However, research has shown that changes to the climate in recent years have not been entirely down to natural causes. It is thought that the actions of people are largely responsible.

 Humans use energy for many different reasons, such as to run our cars and to power the lights in our houses. This energy is largely produced by burning coal, oil and natural gas. Together, these things are known as **fossil fuels**. When these fossil fuels are burnt, they release lots of different gases, which are known as 'greenhouse gases'. One of these greenhouse gases is carbon dioxide.

 The Earth's **atmosphere** is a collection of different gases that surround the planet. The atmosphere allows light and heat from the Sun to pass through to Earth. This makes the planet warm. Some of the light and heat from the Sun bounces off the Earth, travels back through Earth's atmosphere and goes back into space.

 Greenhouse gases mix with the gases in Earth's atmosphere and stop the heat from the Sun bouncing back into space. Because of this, the heat gets trapped inside the Earth's atmosphere. As a result, the temperature on Earth is rising, and this is called global warming. The more greenhouse gases that are released into Earth's atmosphere, the hotter Earth will become.

WHAT ARE WEATHER PATTERNS?

The weather often stays the same for several days. For example, the weather in many countries often stays windy and cold for a few weeks at a time during the winter. Over long periods of time, you can expect to see certain types of weather repeat at certain times of the year. For example, in the United Kingdom (UK) the weather in December is usually cold and rainy, whereas in Australia the weather in December is mostly hot and sunny. When the weather repeats itself and we can follow the repetition, it's called a weather pattern. When the weather stops repeating itself in ways that we can follow, it is known as a weather pattern change.

Bondi Beach in Australia in December

Weather patterns all over the world are recorded by scientists.

Weather patterns and their changes are closely watched by scientists. If weather patterns were to change very suddenly, the world would become a very different place.

Weather Factors

The weather we experience is caused by a number of different **factors**. The first of these is temperature, which is determined by the strength of the Sun's rays. However, the strength of the Sun's rays can be affected by things such as **cloud cover**. If there are lots of clouds in the sky, then less of the Sun's rays reach the ground and the temperature feels cooler.

The amount of **moisture** in the air also affects the weather. Moisture in the air is just tiny water droplets, known as water vapour. The amount of water vapour in the air is called the humidity level. Warm air usually has more moisture in it than cold air, meaning that warm countries usually have higher levels of humidity than cold countries.

Air pressure also affects the weather that we experience. This is because wind is caused by air pressure. Air pressure is quite complicated, but you can think about it as the weight of the air.

The air in our atmosphere can either be under high pressure, which is when it is being pushed together like the air in a balloon, or under low pressure. High-pressure air always wants to move towards low-pressure air.

DIFFERENT
WEATHER PATTERNS

Earth's weather patterns can be broken down into five different types. Each type of weather pattern is found in a different area of the world. The first of these areas are the **polar regions**. For six months of the year, the polar regions experience almost complete darkness and temperatures that fall below -50°C. For the other six months of the year, the Sun shines on these regions, but it is still extremely cold.

The second type of weather pattern can be found in the Earth's temperate zones. Temperate zones are places that experience all four seasons: spring, summer, autumn and winter. These areas have more stable weather conditions than the polar regions, making it much easier for people to live and grow food in these places.

Antarctica is a polar region.

Tropical areas are the opposite of polar regions and they are found around the Earth's **Equator**. Areas around the Equator point almost directly towards the Sun, meaning that it is easier for these places to be warmed by the Sun's rays. As the air is warm, it often has lots of moisture in it, making tropical areas very humid. These areas often experience certain types of extreme weather, such as storms and floods. Tropical areas only have two seasons: wet season and dry season.

Tropical leaves

FIND OUT MORE ABOUT EXTREME WEATHER ON PAGE 18.

Deserts are areas of the world that experience very little rainfall. The temperature in a desert is often very high during the day and very low during the night. Due to the lack of rain in deserts, the air often contains very little moisture. This means there is not enough water in these areas for water vapour to mix with the air.

The final areas of the world that are linked to specific weather patterns are mountainous areas. However, the weather patterns in mountainous areas often change from one **mountain range** to the next. Some mountain ranges tend to experience wind and rain, whereas other mountain ranges tend to be very dry.

Sahara Desert

WHY ARE WEATHER PATTERNS IMPORTANT?

Understanding the different weather patterns on Earth is extremely important. Knowing about different weather patterns helps us to predict the types of weather that might happen in the future. This can help us to do everything from buying sun cream before a sunny day to evacuating a town before a deadly **hurricane** or **monsoon** comes along and destroys it.

Most crops prefer to grow in a certain type of weather. Tomatoes grow best in warm weather, certain types of bamboo prefer to grow high up in mountains and fir trees tend to grow in cold climates. Farmers use weather patterns to help them to decide when to grow different types of crops in order to get the best **yield** from their land.

Tomato plant

Knowing when to expect different types of weather helps to keep people safe. In tropical areas, people prepare for extreme types of weather at times of the year when floods and monsoons are more common. Monitoring weather patterns means that people can be warned about any extreme weather that is likely to hit an area, making it easier for people to take measures to protect themselves.

Warning people about extreme weather before it happens can save lives.

In the past, knowing the weather patterns in your area could mean the difference between life and death. If you know that the yearly rains will start in a few weeks, then you know that now is a good time to plant your seeds. However, you also know not to plant the seeds too close to a river, which could flood and break its banks.

Until 1970, people living near the banks of the River Nile in Africa relied on the weather patterns that caused the river to flood at certain times of the year. The flood waters would destroy any crops or buildings in the way but when the water went away, the soil left behind was perfect for growing crops. However, in 1970 a **dam** was built that has stopped the river from flooding every year.

The people in this village in Egypt are now able to live right next to the River Nile.

WEATHER PATTERNS AND ANIMALS

Humans aren't the only ones to rely on weather patterns. Lots of animals have noticed that the weather repeats itself and they use this knowledge to help them to survive.

Animals that live in temperate zones, which have four seasons, often **migrate** to warmer climates during the winter season. For example, lots of birds migrate because the insects that they eat die in cold weather. The birds fly to warmer regions as their habitat becomes too cold for the insects to survive.

Some animals migrate in order to give birth to their young. Canada geese fly to warmer regions to have their young. If the Canada geese hatched their young in a cold climate, the newly hatched geese might not survive.

These Canada geese are migrating. They can travel up to 965 kilometres (km) in a day.

SEA TURTLES MIGRATE BACK TO THE SAME BEACH THAT THEY WERE HATCHED ON TO LAY THEIR OWN EGGS.

Some animals also use repeating weather patterns to tell them when to hibernate for the winter. Rather than moving to a warmer area, some animals find a warm, dry and safe place to stay hidden during the cold winter. This is called hibernation. They eat plenty of food before they hibernate so that they can survive. Once they are in a warm, safe place, their heart rate slows down and they stay very still to conserve their energy. When the winter is over, the animals come out of hibernation.

Animals rely on repeating weather patterns to know when to start and end their hibernations. When food becomes harder to find, the days get shorter and the nights get colder, animals that hibernate know that it's time to curl up somewhere warm for the winter.

Black bears hibernate during the winter.

Bear cubs are often born during the winter while their mothers are hibernating.

It is important that animals migrate at the correct time. They must time it so that when they arrive in a warmer region, the weather isn't too warm and there is plenty of food. Animals that hibernate must be careful not to hibernate too soon as they may not have enough energy to survive until the end of winter.

WHY ARE WEATHER PATTERNS CHANGING?

*Over the last 200 years, the number of people living on Earth has greatly increased. This rise in **population** has meant that more people are using electricity now than ever before. We use electricity for everything from sending text messages to driving our cars.*

One way of generating electricity is by burning fossil fuels such as coal, oil and gas. Fossil fuels were formed hundreds of millions of years ago. As plants and animals died, rocks and soil slowly covered their remains so that they were buried and tightly squeezed together. This caused the remains of the plants and animals to become very hot and to turn into fossil fuels. Because of this process, huge amounts of fossil fuels are now trapped deep underground.

Coal is a fossil fuel.

Fossil fuels are found under the Earth's surface.

...n fossil fuels are burnt, they release carbon ...de into the atmosphere. Carbon dioxide is ...enhouse gas, meaning that it contributes ...obal warming and climate change. As more ...on dioxide is put into the Earth's atmosphere, ...comes harder for heat from the Sun to leave ...lanet. Greenhouse gases are also produced ...ther things on Earth, including farm animals ...volcanoes. However, the greenhouses gases ...duced from the burning of fossil fuels are ...e of the most damaging to the environment, ...aning that it is important to reduce the amount ...ossil fuels being burnt wherever possible.

As more and more greenhouse gases are released into the atmosphere, it is widely thought that the effects of climate change will get worse. This means that the average temperature on Earth will continue to rise. Global warming is already affecting the weather and things are likely to only get worse if we keep adding more pollutants into the environment and greenhouse gases into the atmosphere. As the weather is also affected by global warming, the weather patterns that are experienced in different areas of the world will also be affected by global warming.

Global warming is affecting weather patterns all around the world.

HOW ARE WEATHER PATTERNS CHANGING?

Global warming is impacting weather patterns by making them more intense. This means that places around the world are likely to carry on experiencing the same types of weather that they did before, just in much more extreme ways.

Global warming is already affecting the weather patterns in Earth's polar regions, which are the coldest places on the planet. The warmer temperatures caused by global warming have caused large areas of ice in the polar regions to melt. These areas of ice have been frozen for hundreds of years, meaning that these areas haven't experienced temperatures as warm as those today in a very long time. If global warming continues to affect the temperature on Earth, these extreme changes in temperature will occur all over the planet.

Global warming is causing a greater number of heatwaves to occur each year. On top of this, the heatwaves seem to be getting hotter and hotter. Heatwaves are long periods of extremely hot weather and, in some cases, very high levels of humidity. The number of heatwaves that have occurred on Earth each year have been monitored for many years and the evidence seems to show that heatwaves are occurring more and more often.

As well as this, some countries are finding that heavy rains are occurring less often. This means the dry periods are lasting longer. This combination of extreme heat and a lack of rainfall has resulted in more droughts and **bushfires** in recent years. Droughts are long periods of very little rainfall. Droughts can cause lots of problems, including damage to crops, which can lead to food shortages. It can also mean there is not enough clean water for drinking, cooking, washing and farming.

EXTREME WEATHER

Global warming seems to be causing an increase in the amount of extreme weather that we experience each year. Extreme weather is any type of weather that is significantly different from the usual, day-to-day weather that a place experiences. Extreme weather is often dangerous and can cause damage to houses and loss of life.

Global warming seems to be affecting the number of hurricanes that the planet experiences each year. A hurricane is a giant storm that has extremely fast winds. Hurricanes form over warm ocean waters. The air above the water gets warmed, which causes it to rise, leaving an area of low air pressure beneath it. More air rushes in to fill this area of low pressure and again it is warmed, which causes it to rise. This process can happen over and over again and can lead to a hurricane. As the temperature on Earth rises, more warm water vapour will rise from the ocean and this will lead to more hurricanes. If a hurricane hits land, it usually brings strong winds, heavy rain and large waves, all of which can be extremely dangerous.

EVERY HURRICANE IS GIVEN A HUMAN NAME, SUCH AS HURRICANE NICOLE, WHICH HAPPENED IN 2016.

Hurricane

As air becomes warmer, it can hold more water vapour. This vapour is eventually released as rain. This means that global warming is causing more heavy rainfalls in some places, which has resulted in flooding. Flooding happens when water flows onto an area of land that would usually be dry. Floods and flash floods can be extremely dangerous and cause lots of damage. A flash flood is a type of flood that happens very quickly, taking people by surprise.

As the water from a flood soaks into the surrounding soil, it loosens the soil and makes it more likely that a landslide will occur.
A landslide is when a large area of earth and rock slides down a hill or mountain. Landslides can destroy natural habitats, bury whole villages and lead to loss of life.

Landslides can be extremely dangerous.

WEATHER PATTERNS IN HISTORY

The climate on Earth has not always stayed the same. Throughout history, there have been lots of changes to the planet's weather patterns. These changes to Earth's climate have had long-lasting effects on the animals and plants that live on the planet.

Millions of years ago, large-scale changes to the Earth's climate and weather patterns began to take place. It is thought that dust from volcanic eruptions and **meteor strikes** was responsible for this. The dust clouds blocked some of the Sun's rays, which caused the temperature on Earth to drop and the weather patterns to change. The clouds also caused some plants and animals to die out.

IT IS THOUGHT THAT A METEOR STRIKE CAUSED THE DINOSAURS TO DIE OUT.

Earth has gone through a number of different ice ages. During each ice age, the Earth becomes very cold and is covered by a thick layer of ice and snow. As the Earth goes through each ice age, some animals manage to do very well while most others die out in the freezing conditions. For example, the woolly mammoth was able to survive the last ice age thanks to its thick coat of fur. It is believed that woolly mammoths survived on some islands until as recently as 4,000 years ago – 8,000 years after the last ice age ended.

There are several different methods that we can use to work out how weather patterns have changed throughout history. One of the most common methods uses the rings on tree trunks. Every year that a tree grows, another ring is formed inside its trunk. Different types of weather can affect the thickness of the ring that a tree produces for that year. This means that by studying the rings of trees growing in similar areas, scientists can work out what the climate was like in that area many years ago.

CASE STUDY: EL NIÑO

*Our oceans and seas affect the Earth's weather patterns more than most people realise. Warm ocean waters can lead to powerful tropical storms and ocean **currents** can lead to certain areas of the world being much warmer or colder than they would be otherwise.*

El Niño is the name given to a natural process that leads to unusually warm ocean waters and increased thunderstorms in certain areas of the Pacific Ocean. During El Niño, winds from the east push the water at the surface of the ocean, which has been warmed by the Sun, to the west. This gives the water just below the surface a chance to be warmed by the Sun, before it too gets blown to the west. As this continues, certain areas of the Pacific Ocean become very warm, often causing numerous thunderstorms to occur. An El Niño event happens around every two to seven years and it is believed to be caused by part of the Pacific Ocean increasing in temperature by just 0.5°C for a period of three months.

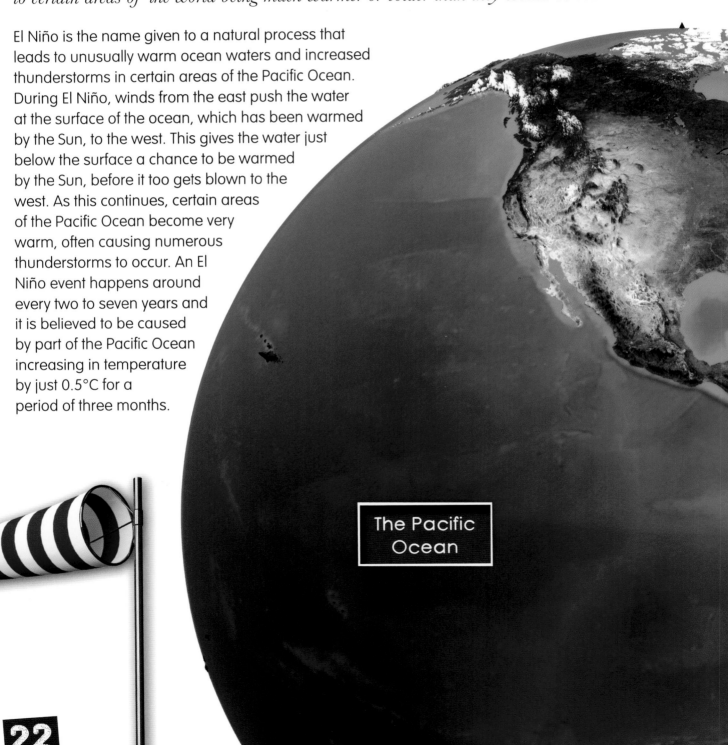

The Pacific Ocean

As all this warm water builds up in certain parts of the Pacific Ocean, it **transfers** heat energy into the air. This causes dramatic changes in weather patterns across North and South America. As warmer air can hold more water vapour, which eventually falls as rain, there is a large increase in the amount of rainfall in the western parts of North and South America. This can often cause dangerous flash floods. These areas also experience storms and **tornadoes** that can be extremely dangerous. In Australia and Southeast Asia, the opposite happens. These places often experience extreme droughts and bushfires.

Tornado

THE BIGGEST EL NIÑO EVENT EVER RECORDED HAPPENED BETWEEN 1997 AND 1998. THE IMPACTS OF THIS EVENT INCLUDED EXTREME HEATWAVES AND RECORD-BREAKING FLOODS.

for w   is t
to be best in
point of vie
El Nino
climatic e
warming o
catastropl
for wha

Scientists are getting better at predicting when an El Niño event will take place, which helps people to plan for the extreme types of weather that it causes.

THE GULF STREAM

The Gulf Stream is a strong and fast-moving current of water in the Atlantic Ocean. Water that gets warmed in the Gulf of Mexico flows all the way up the east coast of North America and across the Atlantic Ocean. Here it splits, with one part flowing around northern Europe and other flowing down the west coast of Africa, eventually circling back west to its starting point in the Gulf of Mexico. The Gulf Stream is partly caused by winds that force the water to move in certain directions. Although there are many different currents in the Earth's oceans, the Gulf Stream is one of the most important due to the impact that it has on the climate.

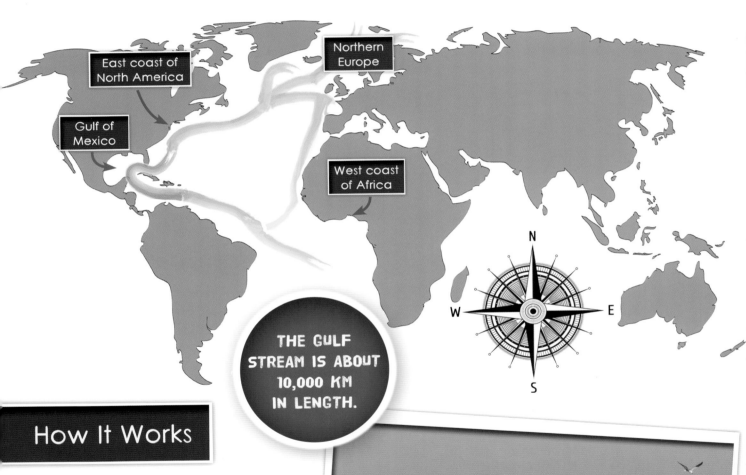

East coast of North America

Northern Europe

Gulf of Mexico

West coast of Africa

THE GULF STREAM IS ABOUT 10,000 KM IN LENGTH.

How It Works

Ocean water in the Gulf of Mexico is warmed by the Sun before beginning its journey towards Europe. This warm water warms the air above it, causing changes in the climate. The warm water helps to make places in northern Europe, such as the UK, warmer than normal.

The climate in the Gulf of Mexico is very warm and the waters are very shallow. This makes it easy for the water in the Gulf of Mexico to be warmed by the Sun.

Although it is impossible to say for certain, many scientists believe that global warming will have a huge effect on the Gulf Stream. **Glaciers** are slowly melting because of the increase in the Earth's temperature caused by global warming. Many scientists believe that, as the glaciers melt into the Gulf Stream in the northern Atlantic Ocean, it will make the water colder, and this will effect the temperature in northern Europe and western Africa.

IT IS ESTIMATED THAT, WITHOUT THE GULF STREAM, THE TEMPERATURE IN THE UK WOULD DROP BY AROUND 5°C.

Studies have shown that the strength of the Gulf Stream is beginning to slow down and become weaker. If the Gulf Stream was to stop flowing completely, it would change the climate and usual weather patterns for many places all around the world.

HOW CAN WE PREDICT FUTURE WEATHER?

Meteorologists use a variety of methods to predict what the weather will be like in the future. There are weather stations all around the world that are constantly measuring things such as the outside temperature and wind speed. These weather stations send this information back to the meteorologists so that they can work out the weather conditions in different locations. Other factors, such as the humidity level, are measured by **buoys** out at sea.

The buoys float on top of the ocean and record information about the weather in the area.

Floating around in space are weather **satellites**. Different satellites do different jobs; some take pictures of the clouds, while others measure the amount of rainfall. By looking at all the information together, meteorologists can work out the types of weather that certain places can expect to experience in the coming hours and days.

Satellite

We now know a lot about weather patterns, as well as how different types of weather are created and the things that can affect the weather. We have lots of different machines, measuring devices and satellites that help us to predict the weather in the future. However, even with all this knowledge and all these new types of technology, predicting the weather is still extremely difficult. This is because too many different things can affect the weather, meaning that it can go from beautiful sunshine to heavy rain in only a few minutes. Even though we now know a lot about the causes and effects of different types of weather, it is still very difficult to be certain about what the weather will be like in the future.

Scientists will continue to study the ways in which global warming changes the Earth.

The same thinking applies to global warming. We now know a lot about global warming and how it is currently affecting our planet. We also know what many of the main causes of global warming are, such as pollution and burning fossil fuels. However, we still do not know for certain how global warming and climate change will affect our planet in the future.

A careful balance of air pressure, wind, temperature and humidity is causing the weather in your area right now. In the same way, a balance between the greenhouse gas levels in our atmosphere, the rate at which glaciers are melting and the Earth's temperature will determine the effects of global warming.

HOW CAN WE HELP?

There are lots of different ways that we can help to slow down the rate of climate change and look after our planet.

Tell your family and friends all about climate change and how important it is to look after our planet.

Find out about any **conservation** work happening in your area and try to get people interested in helping too.

Try to reduce the amount of fossil fuels that you use. Rather than using the car, try to walk or cycle to where you want to go. If you must use a car, try sharing with friends who are going to the same place. You could also turn down the heating at home and wear more layers of clothing to stay warm instead.

4 Recycle! It is important that we recycle as much as possible in order to reduce the amount of waste we produce. Many things made of plastic, glass and paper can be recycled, so try to make sure that everything you can recycle is taken to special recycling banks or put in recycling bins.

Plant a tree! Trees **absorb** some of the greenhouse gases that cause climate change. The more trees that are planted, the better. **5**

The WWF hold 'Earth Hour' every year. On the last Saturday in March, everyone who is taking part turns off the lights in their house for one hour between 8:30 pm and 9:30 pm. The WWF hope that this act will show how much people care about the planet. Why not join in and turn off your lights for an hour?

FUN FACTS

IN 2015, IT RAINED IN A VILLAGE IN WALES FOR 83 DAYS IN A ROW.

HUNDREDS OF THUNDERSTORMS ARE HAPPENING AROUND THE WORLD RIGHT NOW!

EYE

THE eye OF A HURRICANE CAN BE OVER 300 KM WIDE.

THE LARGEST SNOWBALL FIGHT ON RECORD TOOK PLACE IN CANADA IN 2016. 7,681 PEOPLE CAME TOGETHER TO THROW SNOWBALLS AT EACH OTHER!

EVERY MINUTE, AROUND ONE BILLION TONNES OF RAIN FALLS ONTO EARTH.

GLOSSARY

absorb — to take in or soak up

atmosphere — the mixture of gases that make up the air and surround the Earth

buoys — floating markers in the ocean

bushfires — fires that spread rapidly in areas such as forests

cloud cover — the amount of cloud in the sky

conservation — work that is done to protect something from damage or harm

currents — steady flows of water in one direction

dam — a human-made structure built across a river to hold back the water

Equator — the imaginary line around the Earth that is an equal distance from the North and South Poles

eye — the calm region at the centre of a storm or hurricane

factors — things that influence an outcome or result

fossil fuels — fuels, such as coal, oil and gas, that formed millions of years ago from the remains of animals and plants

glaciers — large masses of ice that move very slowly

hurricane — a violent storm with a strong wind that moves in a circle

meteor strikes — when small bodies of matter from outer space strike Earth

meteorologists — scientists who study weather

migrate — move from one place to another based on seasonal changes

moisture — liquid in the form of very small drops

monsoon — a pattern of strong winds that blow through southern Asia

mountain range — a group of connected mountains

polar regions — areas surrounding the North and South Poles

population — the number of people living in a place

satellites — machines in space that travel around planets, take photographs and collect and transmit information

tornadoes — fast-moving, strong and destructive winds that form into funnel shapes

transfers — moves from one place to another

volcanic eruptions — when steam and other material violently leaves a volcano

yield — the amount produced

INDEX